Resurrection

The Song of Silence

AJ

BookLeaf Publishing

India | USA | UK

Presentation by *BookLeaf Publishing*

Web: www.bookleafpub.com

E-mail: info@bookleafpub.com

ISBN: 9789358361698

First edition 2021

"To chosen family."

1. "the body is a poem

to be unpicked

unlocked

devoured

yet- most of all-

to be (mis)interpreted.

after all,

the writing on my skin

can only be read by the trained eye

my life is engraved on the very essence of me

(which i wish i could destroy)

patterns of scars read like braille

understood by me alone.

my body is a work (in progress)

a poem.

not perfect yet,

it must be hidden away.

trace me,

read my story.

don't come too close,

after all, paper is fragile:

handle with care."

2. "I'm eating my words

As they dance on my tongue

Making me squirm as they turn

Oh- I'm biting I'm chewing

(Simply swallowing my pride)

They pin me-

Puncturing my mind-

As I sit here in silence

(Muted like a mime)

I can't say it. I fear it.

The version that you'll see-

If I emit all of these feelings-

My caged memories: they haunt me;

They taunt me.

Like a stained porcelain tub

(You can't rid it of residue

No matter how hard you scrub)

That's my mind;

They're my eyes:

Tinted-

As eroded as these beaches.

I'm drowning from you.

Your fingers-

They've grabbed me

Now bruising my soul

How can one escape from your grasp?

I just long to feel whole.

See-

these visions you've gifted me

Were your most vicious curse."

3. "Please, don't let the morning come.

The sun goes down, but the words stay hung.

(Please, don't let the morning come.)

Rest your head, close your eyes-

Maybe listen to my lullaby?

Be still,

For if you move, the shadow comes.

It hurts like hell;

It clouds the sky;

It never goes, but it sometimes hides.

Didn't you listen to the lullaby?

You're supposed to close your eyes.

(Please, don't let the morning come)

I beg for noise;

Pray for silence.

(Please, don't let the morning come.)

Now lay me down to sleep,

I pray to God you don't hear me weep.

(Please, don't let the morning come.)

There's supposed to be a lullaby-

Up comes the sun, as I drift off to sleep.

Please, God...

 I feel so weak.

(Please, don't let the morning come.)"

4. "Follow me into my world-

Just for a moment-

I know I can't explain myself-

As much as I might try.

'Cause:

I'm so beyond broken

That I forget

How to even Breathe...

Words choke me from the inside out-

As if voices are screaming:

You will choke,

(Hands around your throat)

You will convulse.

She is speaking in tongues,

Yet the rambling is clear.

She traces my breaths

(And hesitant steps)

Willing me to disappear:

Control the uncontrollable

Count to infinity

Capture smoke with bare hands.

So,

Every day I try and try to just

Try.

I want to show you how I feel but

I can't move (Even an inch)

From this empty hole in my mind:

Dragging me deeper and deeper...

Every day I try and try to just

Try.

But I can't anymore.

After being abandoned so many times

(I learnt to live on my own; relying on myself to
survive)

I forgot how to trust:

In anyone else, let alone my own mind.

I'm fighting the knife that my own hand wields;

Fighting hands that are clenched round my throat.

My conditioned mind cannot be trusted:

What I feel may (not) exist.

It's safer to care less

Where I feel

Nothing.

Where I am

Nothing but a mirror-

shattered-

Reflecting

Someone who once was.

Now, I have nothing to lose.

Except the skin on my back;

the words which I carve-

With a delicate touch-

Onto my skin

(Onto my soul)

To hide

The bruises-

Make beauty out of pain.

Now, I'm so beyond broken-

I can't speak these words.

But spew acid instead-

Burning my own skin

With the toxicity built up

Within."

5. "This is the last line of the poem.

You got there

Without even realising it...

Because this poem rhymes.

You just missed it.

Go back-

Check.

You still don't understand?

Well, you're delusional.

It rhymes; it's a sonnet-

Sonnets rhyme.

You are not all there, trust me-

It's in iambic pentameter.

Just because

You don't understand,

Don't try to make

Me

The villain.

It would be so hurtful-

Especially since I'm helping you:

Let me help you.

You think you know better than me...

I'm the poem.

You must be:

Insanely arrogant;

Extremely cruel;

Mildly insane;

Simply psychotic;

To think

You

Know better than

Me.

You aren't even reading me.

(We already established that)

You. Aren't. Reading. This. Poem.

It's about butterflies;

As the first line says,

"Why would I lie?""

6. "I don't know why

I bother with my voice,

A soft, pale thing,

That doesn't stretch,

No, it falls far and fast

And quietly.

I can't bring myself to

A single utterance

Worth my breath

And the world's time -

God!

There is no time to be

Loud and brash and fiery.

Not when you can seethe

Silently.

They say a choking throat

Shuts you up.

If so then

Will a slit to my throat

Let my voice pour out

Like cold, sad blood?"

7. "Was I cursed at birth

to live on the brink of death?

Trapped in this trance...

The fear of a hundred voices asking me why-

Why oh why do I want to die?

Well, I wish to mute the agony,

execute my destiny,

see daylight:

please-it's meant to be.

You can't stop me.

Plath said it best-

I do it well,

my scars can attest.

Perhaps I'm not as strong as I once thought:

I fear I am nature's mistake.

For the hands of fate,

I must partake in this sacrifice to begin my demise.

(This shouldn't come as a surprise)."

8. "Martin Luther King did not say I have a strategic plan;

He said

'I have a dream'

I too have a dream

A wish

A hope

A life to live.

For, though the caged bird may sing,

It is the free bird that has a song.

The doors may all be shut-

One after another

Slammed in my face,

But not all closed doors are locked.

Sometimes you have to pus,

To move,

To act,

To do

(alohomora should do it)

After all,

Happiness can be found

In the darkest of times;

But Dumbledore had magic to turn on the lights.

And in this mad,

Futuristic

(suffocating)

World:

We still do not.

We still do not.

Instead-we have to move, to act, to do

To activate these effing motion sensor lights.

Sometimes we must treat life as an exercise in creative writing.

We cannot write a new beginning;

We can change the end.

If only it were so simple…

Instead its an exercise in continuous prose.

Do not lift up the pen,

Do not stop,

Do not breathe.

No. Stop. Breathe.

If you don't swim, you won't drown.

You may splutter and flail

But you do not need to fall victim to all these

'Inspirational' phrases

You do not need a strategic plan-

You need a song, a dream, a hope, a life to live, a
reason to fight.

It's not meant to be a war-

But when it rains it pours.

Ha- I will not be conquered by something as trivial
as the weather,

I'm used to it for its not just the wind that wails.

Sometimes when you fall, you fall forwards.

The grazes seem to be trophies of the enemies you've vanquished,

No matter big or small.

And, how do you stand up?

Not with a strategic plan:

You put one foot in front of the other

And learn to walk-

Again.

9. "capital letters scare me.

 i am not assertive

(enough)

to use them.

because...

they declare

audacity.

the words grow in my head

that i am too afraid to speak

(aloud)

forcing me to crouch in the corner

desperately seeking an escape from the confines of
this body:

hide away

(they say)

shrink away.

because-

how can you take up space in a room?

how can you have the audacity to be?

it's easier to make yourself tiny;

sacrifice your voice before it's stolen;

carved out from your throat leaving an ugly scar

which speaks louder than i ever could.

so now,

i cry because you wouldn't let me speak

i speak because you wouldn't let me scream

i scream because you wouldn't let me

be

anything to you."

10. "and in that deafening silence,

i've never wished more to be heard,

wracked with endless demurs of regret and
remorse –

impure, impure, impure."

11. "Laid upon the tiles, asleep in the rusted tub

with a tear-stained face;

red-lighting bolts in her sunken eyes;

scars on her flaked skin:

let the afterlife begin.

Do I perish with fingers entwined

a few whispers of false goodwill

in my casket I will lay

fixed, flawless, perfect

a wax being

awaiting celestial magic

(or Heaven

or Hell

or nothing)

who knows how much this life weighs?

Ha! Never mind

this is only a reckless fantasy

a way to elude one's own reality."

12. "My heart isn't broken

it's bruised

like a map across my skin;

across my soul;

across my body:

a black ocean,

swallowing me whole.

Now,

itt hurts to be touched

(watch me beg for more)

it hurts to be loved

(watch me try anyway)

Watch my skin crawl, as my fingertips caress my fractured body;

look at the footprints they leave behind.

Stare into my bloodshot eyes:

tell me it was my fault;

tell me I bruised myself;

tell me I hammered my own heart against the inside
of my rib cage-

until the only thing left beating was my fists against
my chest

(a cheap imitation for the beating of a heart)

Believe me when I tell you

that I no longer ache for you.

for every old bruise

is shaped like your fingertips-

when these bruises fade

new ones will take their place.

I hope they hurt;

I hope they're beautiful."

13. "You always knew it would happen again:

the whispered code, the silhouettes, and then

a muffled crunch, a stifled cough, a soft and cryptic knock.

A latch that wasn't fastened on a door that didn't lock.

They'll catch you, they'll break you,

they'll wipe you for sure.

They know your every step and stop:

where you are, where you'll be,

exactly where you were.

What did you feel when your mind was removed;

was it hard, sharp and painful, or satiny smooth?

Do you weep in the dark, do you know in your heart

that they kept you intact when they tore you apart?

Does your lurching awareness obsess on your doom,

do those tiptoeing whispers leave prints in your room?

Keep moving, keep hiding, till death brings the end.

They're just around the corner, they're just around the bend.

Go leap out the window, go slip through the trees,

burn the leaves in your journal and bury your keys.

Haunt the alleys and rails as you sneak town to town;

one eye on your back, one eye on the ground.

So where was your head when they rewrote your brain.

Did you think you were God, a file, or insane.

Are you groping for clues in the patterns they weave—

is a single thing real in the world you perceive.

They're coming. Keep running. Don't let yourself fall behind.

They're searching through your blackest dreams, escorted by the blind.

They're watching from the shadows, their burning eyes aligned.

They're waiting in the dark around the corner of your mind."

14. "I'd like to tell you a story,

A thrilling tale,

So gather round;

Listen up;

Don't fall asleep

(You'll miss the twist).

Try to solve

A murder.

It's no average brain teaser;

No psychological trick;

There are no prizes for guessing,

But you might just get a kick.

For ,

There once was a murder,

But this one has a twist-

The victim was my innocence:

Stolen was my bliss.

There was no crime scene;

No yellow tape,

No blood,

No gore-

For souls do not bleed,

And my body was not left on the floor.

The only evidence left

Were fingerprints on my soul.

The only witnesses-

My own two eyes.

(Not exactly trustworthy,

Since they didn't see through the lies)

Have you figured it out yet?

Or do you need more time?

More clues?

I'll indulge you

(For a while)

You can revel in my murder-

As if it is a game,

Not the source of all my pain.

There were no clues-

not a single trace.

Except for the memories inside me,

Which I can never erase.

No weapon left abandoned,

For words don't leave a mark,

Bruises are easily covered

And no one cares for scars.

They never found a body

(Nor did they find my soul)

I'm a prisoner in my own skin,

For this wasn't a normal murder-

Oh, why can't they see-

The girl inside my body,

Is no longer me.

There never was a funeral,

Because no one knew I died.

I guess that's just what happens,

When you keep it all inside.

So, roll up,

Roll up to see-

To stare and speculate.

Did you solve my murder?

Or will I continue to wait...?"

15. "To be practised are the things to better within myself, I must work my gifts

For if too long they lie there stagnant, eventually they'll be missed. It's been forever since I can remember a poem of mine with run-on lines. I can't remember to, mustn't, but I want to, reality's wrong but otherwise, I'm fine

Going about my daily lives, I strive to make me better than the best. Expectations of perfection, I can't care, I can never be less-

Concerning all that I am learning, getting, being, staying here

Hides an appreciation of my disassociations, my delusions, don't hug me, I am scared

It's been a while since I last smiled at a prose of mine made out of deliberation

A fever dream, I scream through my glass casket to a denying nation. Let me out-

it festers, a pest, I confess to the caging of a tiger

Repression, suppression well sedation, I'm deduced, I am a (or rather the) liar

I live to love, I hate to live, But love- a reality; people nonexistent

No matter what happens, as things get out of hand,
it stands, the maddening's consistent

Can't see the wrong, just as I'm taught, you
awaken, to fix the mixed, you're seeking

Asleep I lie, waiting to die, everything's alright is all
I see, I be to once denied, unwanted memories,
unstopping, ever fleeting."

16. "I can't let you touch my body;

I don't love with my body-

never will-

and my heart is still part of my flesh

(I'm sorry)

but,

(if you'd like)

there's still my mind.

perhaps you cannot explore

every hidden inch of my skin,

I'll let you indulge into my my deepest secrets-

joys and sorrows;

loves and fears

memories...

I would bare all.

there's still my spirit;

there's still my soul-

I can think of no better intimacy. are you asking for my everything?

what greater gift can I give?

in return you could give me yours-

together

we could form a bond like no other:

share an intimacy that is

totally untouchable."

17. "Sometimes,

I do not pray for answers or actions.

There is:

No bequest requested.

No grant, no teach,

No need or greed asked.

Just a:

Hey! Listen up!

This is a prayer

That my eyes only utter.

My tongue

(self-silenced)

Can only watch

And must approve.

In fact,

This is more of a PSA

Than a prayer,

Updating you-

Heavenly Father-

On the state of

What we earth temporaries call

Heart, mind and soul;

And even your diligently designed,

Crafted carrier:

My body.

I ask for no interference

From the sidelines.

Neither from the

Mother sky

That raised me up gloriously this lifetime;

Nor from the earth

That this day

Gives me sustenance,

As much spiritual

As grained cereal delights.

I'm learning still to live

With my means,

Such as they are,

Sometimes mean.

Yet you granted me this skill:

To express.

This prayer is one of gratitude.

Though gratitude comes and goes

Like summer breezes,

In this moment I do pray.

My heart, my mind, my soul

Drink inspiration from the sky

(the blue glue of our

Common delighted,

Uncommon existence.)

This skill is

At this moment

Mine.

Yet,

My failing, flailing skills

Cannot help express

In new ways,

A gratitude that has a

shapeless shape.

For prayers are of gratitude

Are instantaneous fulfilled,

And thus granted even before

They are completed."

18. "An acrid heat

Rises in my vocal cords.

It tells me to do things I don't want to do;

But I do want to-

I just wish

I didn't.

It steals my voice,

Whispers manipulations;

Masquerades as my saviour.

It reminds me

How sweetly it stings

When I drag my fingers

Against my skin.

How could I say no?

It begs me to do more,

Hurt more.

It wants me to hurt

(I want to hurt)

I(t) want(s me) to hurt.

'It' Never was anything

But my own desires.

I just don't want them

To be

Mine.

19. "'It's time you start writing about your psychosis'

That's what I was told.

But,

I have a journal of dreams

(that I may or may not have had)

Inside my journal:

Pieces of my body;

Flowers;

A to-do list with nothing crossed off;

There are pictures over every word

(disguised in a metaphor)

I can't remember the language to describe.

Expression makes the most sense when you are

Expressing the bad.

This is eruption-

A compulsion that is combusting

From my pencil into black ink.

'So I don't have to'

My psychosis is in every line.

It is in my eyes darting back and forth.

I write so much the page turns black.

My psychosis is:

The shadow trail behind every letter;

It is the blood coming out of my mouth

(when I say I'll do better)

The scratches on my hands and feet are from
holding on too tight

To demons that know how to fight back.

It is my teeth, and the holes inside of them, spit on
the page.

I wince. I turn the page.

I try to say it so many times it becomes
meaningless

You wouldn't believe me if I told you.

I spit again,

My mind looks like a minefield and these words are
just the smoke.

45

20. "Resurrection:

A celebration of the way

We rise

From our darkness,

Digressions,

Failures,

Weakness,

Sadness

(and depressions)

He teaches me to subdue the anger-

Every hint of violence inside-

To be true to the unique creature his

Father has crafted-

True to my own voice.

Unlike Jesus,

I am not that courageous and mighty with the power
of love.

I am unlike Jesus in too many ways,

But I am like him in my rising from darkness and doom,

From my own self-made tomb.

My resurrections might be tiny;

Large is the Spirit in me,

The ability to see the Light,

To see the Right-

Pursue it wherever it leads.

I tell my little stories

From death

To glory."